Eating Clean

100 Appetizing Solutions for Wheat-Free and Dairy-Free Meals

Lisa Allen

Foreword by Dr. Sara Thyr
Recipes Edited by Dr. Sara Thyr

❧ MORNING GLORY PRESS • NEW HAMPSHIRE

EATING CLEAN

100 Appetizing Solutions for Wheat-Free and Dairy Free Meals
by Lisa Allen

Published by:
MORNING GLORY PRESS
Post Office Box 373
Nashua NH 03061-0373 U.S.A.

http://a-zmarketing.com

Book Design & Production by Lisa Allen
Cover photo by DeCicco Photography
Recipe Editing by Sara Thyr, N.D.
Proofreading & Copyediting by Wendy Flynn

ISBN, print ed.   0-9722477-0-X

First Printing: August, 2002

Printed in the United States of America

Thank you to everyone who believed in the usefulness of this project, who encouraged me along the way, and who experienced vicariously the birth of an idea into a book.
You know who you are! Thank you.

CONTENTS

FOREWORD

There is a fine line in the practice of medicine between asking your patients to do what you know will be most beneficial to them, and giving them a task that is too daunting. Never is this line more vibrant than when I ask patients to work on detoxification, and even making some healthful diet changes. They will derive great benefit if they can eat exceptionally clean. But our society doesn't readily support this notion. And many patients don't even know where to begin, even if they are willing.

This is what I faced when I asked my patient Lisa to do a detox a year ago. She was willing, but wanted more than steamed broccoli and brown rice to eat. I didn't have a good recipe resource for her, and thus an idea was born. Lisa's love for cooking, books and publishing have brought forth an exceptional guide for patients who need to detoxify their bodies, or who just want to eat more healthfully as they go through life.

The recipes given here are healthful, simple, and delicious. They can be added to and altered as one feels the creative urge. I suggest buying organic ingredients whenever possible. The problems associated with the pesticides, hormones, and chemicals in non-organic food are too numerous to mention here. But the alarming increase in cancer rates in this country is a vivid reflection of the problem.

I know that there are as many methods of doing a detoxification as there are practitioners. I tend to mean "liver detoxification" when I say detox to my patients. And you will notice comments in the book about foods that are known to be particularly good for the liver.

Ideas in this book are not set in stone. They are suggestions for improvement. Many of the ingredients will be controversial, and the best advice I can give is that you listen to your healthcare practitioner and modify ingredients as your needs require. I find that most importantly we need to make sure that people are supporting their liver, eliminating efficiently, and not adding any further toxins to their bodies. This is another reason to eat organically, especially on a detox. (Turn to page 130 for the Envirnomental Working Group's list of the "Dirty Dozen" most toxic fruits and vegetables; this can help you decide where to spend your organic dollar.) You can also substitute tofu when you see chicken in a recipe, if you are avoiding all meat.

It is always a delight to be part of the process of people on the road to greater wellness. I am so happy to have this book to offer to patients and colleagues as a tool for healthful and tasty eating on that path.

Sara Thyr, N.D.

BREAKFAST

IDEAS

BREAKFAST AT TIFFANY'S

dry hot rice cereal
water
½ cup non-dairy bever-
　age: soy, almond or rice
　milk
¼ cup blueberries, fresh
　is better

Prepare a single serving of the hot cereal according to directions. While that is cooking, put non-dairy beverage and blueberries into a glass only bowl. (Plastics can release when microwaved.) Heat combination in the microwave for 1-2 minutes. (If you've just taken your soy milk out of the fridge, for example, it will take longer to heat than if you've just opened a new container off the shelf.) Now add the cereal. Top with a few more fresh berries and serve.

This was my first 'creation' when I began my first detox. I was very excited to discover that I could eat 'real food' that looked and tasted good, too. I hope you'll find it delicious, filling and very satisfying, as well.

IMMUNE SUPPORT BREAKFAST

"This is a well-known naturopathic recommendation.
It should be noted, however, that it is not configured to be
hypoallergenic."   — Dr. Sara Thyr

4 cups rolled grains
2 cups oat bran
½ cup dried fruit
1 cup sunflower seeds
(may be ground)
1 cup nuts, raw & unsalted
1 cup lecithin granules
1 cup flax seed (ground is recommended)
1 cup silybum marianum seeds (commonly known as Milk Thistle; grinding required)

Flax seed, sunflower seeds and Milk Thistle may be available already ground from your health food store. If not, grind each of these separately. Measuring out the recipe amounts indicated at left, mix all of the breakfast ingredients together in a large mixing bowl. Stir thoroughly. Store in an airtight container in the refrigerator.

PREPARATION:

Soak ½ cup (per serving) for at least 30 minutes in water, soy milk or nut milk. For extra sweetness, add a sliced banana or peach just before serving. Soak the mixture the night before and simplify your morning routine. Enjoy a quick breakfast or, include some in your brown bag lunch for a mid-morning energy treat.

OATMEAL CEREAL

hot oatmeal cereal
1 teaspoon cinnamon
dash of nutmeg
2 Tbs. raisins

½ cup non-dairy beverage:
  soy, almond or rice milk
1 Tbs. molasses (optional)

Prepare a single serving of oatmeal according to package directions. While the oats are cooking, stir in the raisins, cinnamon and nutmeg.

Heat the soy, almond or rice milk in the microwave for 1-2 minutes.

Spoon oatmeal into a bowl, pour heated milk (and molasses, if you choose) over it, and serve.

POACHED PRUNES and HOT BREAKFAST CEREAL

My father discovered the sweet satisfaction of poached prunes when he was forced to give up more conventional treats. So excited about them, was he, that he often served Poached Prunes as a dessert when having guests for lunch or dinner. We've brought them to the breakfast table. Enjoy!

3 – 6 dried and pitted prunes
¼ – ½ tsp. cinnamon
nutmeg – just a dash

Cream of Rice Cereal or Oatmeal
¼ cup soy, nut or rice milk

Place the prunes, cinnamon, nutmeg in a small saucepan and add enough water to cover the prunes. Bring to a simmer. Reduce heat to low, cover, and continue to simmer for 20 more minutes.

When the prunes are almost done, prepare the hot cereal. Then, garnish with prunes and embellish with soy, nut or rice milk.

Toast & Go!

2 slices Rice or Spelt
Bread, toasted
1 Tbs. Almond butter
pure and unsweetend,
preservative-free
1 Tbs. **Fruit & Nut
Spread** (see page 108)

Spread a layer of almond butter and then the fruit & nut spread on each slice of toasted rice or spelt bread. An easy and healthful breakfast (or mini meal) that travels well, too.

DRINKS

ALMOND MILK

A homemade alternative to store-bought and a good way to prepare raw almonds for eating.

2 cups raw almonds
water, distilled, to cover
4 – 6 dates

cheese cloth or fine-
  mesh strainer

In a generous-sized bowl, cover almonds with the distilled water. Add the dates. Allow nuts and dates to soak for 12 hours.

Using a piece of cheese cloth or a fine-mesh strainer, strain off and save the liquid. You now have homemade Almond Milk. Refrigerate any Almond Milk that you do not consume right away.

NOTE: Nuts that have been prepared this way are easier for your body to digest. Dry, they are in a dormant, seed-like state that inhibits enzyme absorption. After soaking they can be considered a 'live food' and nutrients are fully accessible to your body.

COCONUT MILK

Homemade and Unprocessed

3 cups boiling water
1 cup unsweetened
coconut (freshly grated
is the best or purchase
it prepackaged from
health food store)

1 large square cheese-
cloth (commonly found
at most supermarkets)

Place coconut in a large
mixing bowl. Pour the
boiling water over it and
allow the coconut to set
for 20 minutes.

Strain the entire mixture
through cheesecloth into
another bowl or container,
squeezing all of the mois-
ture from the coconut
flakes.

Use immediately.
Refrigerate leftovers.

BANANA BERRY SMOOTHIE

Save over-ripe bananas in the freezer and you'll always have ingredients ready for this healthy fruity alternative to the traditional milk shake. The consistency of the frozen banana is not unlike ice cream, making this a refreshing hot-weather treat.

---

1 frozen banana

¼ cup blueberries, fresh or frozen

1 cup non-dairy beverage: soy, almond or rice milk

1 Tbs. 'Green Food' (optional)

¼ cup vanilla whey protein powder (optional)

PUBLISHER S UPDATE:
Please use soy-based protein powder, not whey-based.

In a blender, puree together the banana, blueberries and non-dairy beverage until thick and smooth.

If you like, add Green Food powder and/or the vanilla whey powder. Puree again until well blended.

Turn to page 133 for a word from Dr. Thyr about Green Food.

TRIPLE BERRY BLEND

Another Protein Smoothie

¼ cup blueberries, fresh or frozen

½ cup organic (see the dirty dozen list) strawberries, fresh or frozen

¼ cup raspberries, fresh or frozen

1 cup non-dairy beverage: soy, almond or rice milk

¼ cup whey protein powder (vanilla flavored)

PUBLISHER S UPDATE:
Please use soy-based protein powder, not whey-based.

In a blender, puree fruit and non-dairy beverage. Then add protein powder and blend thoroughly.

Serve immediately.

TASTE HINT: If you use only fresh berries, either add an ice cube or two to the blender when mixing, or fill the glass with ice before serving.

TROPICAL POWER DRINK

1 cup coconut milk
(see pg. 20)
½ cup pineapple chunks,
fresh
½ cup mango chunks,
fresh or frozen
¼ cup whey-based pro-
tein powder
2 - 3 ice cubes (to taste)
½ banana (optional)
1 Tbs. Green Food
(optional)

Blend all ingredients until completely smooth and irresistible. Drink immediately!

PUBLISHER S UPDATE:
Please use soy-based protein powder, not whey-based.

"This should be a daily drink for those on a detox, and for anyone who isn't, it's a wonderful treat."
— Dr. Thyr

PROTEIN SMOOTHIE

½ cup mango chunks, fresh or frozen

¼ cup blueberries, fresh or frozen

1 cup non-dairy beverage: soy, almond or rice milk

¼ cup soy-based protein powder

1 Tbs. 'Green Food'

In a blender, puree fruit and non-dairy beverage. Then add powders and blend thoroughly. Serve immediately.

Turn to page 133 for a word from Dr. Thyr about Green Food.

PINEAPPLE JUICE

Before traveling to Brazil, I had never even thought about making pineapple juice in my own kitchen. Of course, there's something exotic and exciting about picking the pineapple off the tree. But even if the only fresh pineapple available to you is at the local grocery, this juice is a delight.

1 ripe pineapple
Xylitol, to taste
water, as needed

Wash off the outside of the pineapple and pat dry with paper towel. Slice off the bottom and discard, so that the pineapple can rest on your cutting board in an upright position, while you hold the leaves on the top like a handle. Working around the outside of the fruit, from top to bottom, slice off the skin and discard. Then, cut off the leafy top and discard. Slice the pineapple into sections and cut into chunks no larger than 2". Put some of these chunks into the blender. Add water. Working in batches, puree pineapple pieces with water. After each batch is pureed, pour it through a kitchen sieve into a large bowl.

(continued on page 26)

Press the pulp against the mesh so that you get every delicious drop!

Once all of the pineapple chunks have been pureed, you can begin to sweeten the juice with the Xylitol. Sweetness is a personal preference. Start with a small amount of xylitol and continue to taste and add sweetener until you achieve perfection.

Delicious served at room temperature, over ice, or chilled.

NOTE: Pineapple juice will lose its fresh flavor after two days in the fridge and will go bad soon after.

ABOUT **XYLITOL**:

Xylitol is made from xylose, a 5-carbon sugar that is derived from fibrous plants. It is often synthesized from corn, but other sources may be used. There are some great studies showing benefit in preventing dental carries, and using it as a spray to treat sinus infections. It is generally acceptable for use during a liver detox, but check with your naturopath first before using. Xylitol will not cause your blood sugar to spike and is a recommended alternative for those who struggle to maintain a consistent blood sugar count. See individual containers for caloric and further nutritional detail.

Main Dishes

and Entrees

CALIFORNIA ROLLS

4 sheets of roasted seaweed (known as "Nori"; available in oriental groceries, health food stores and the international section of larger supermarkets)

1 avocado, peeled and sliced
1 cucumber, peeled and seeded
3 cups rice, cooked
4 tsp. roasted sesame seeds
8 Tbs. shredded crab meat or steamed and chopped shrimp (optional)

DIPPING SAUCE:

¼ cup wheat free soy or tamari sauce
¼ scallion, sliced thinly
1 tsp. sesame oil

Cut cucumber into lengths equal to the width of the seaweed sheets (usually 7"). Then slice each section, lengthwise, into quarters.

On a single sheet of the seaweed, spread ½ cup of rice. Sprinkle 1 tsp. of sesame seeds over the rice. An inch in from the edge closest to you, place 2 pieces of cucumber, 2 pieces avocado, and 2 Tbs. crab meat or shrimp. Fold up the 1" edge onto the fillings and begin to roll the seaweed sheet as you would a sleeping bag. Continue until you have a delightful roll. Repeat 3 more times, to make 4 rolls. With a sharp knife, cut each roll into 6-8 slices.

In a small dish, combine tamari sauce, scallion and sesame oil and serve with your California Rolls!

MANDARIN SALAD

2 cups romaine lettuce, rinsed, dried and torn into pieces

1 orange, peeled; sections cut into bite-size chunks

2 – 3 slices red onion

½ cup fresh snap or snow peas

2 tsp. toasted sesame seeds

Assemble salad ingredients. Dress with **Mandarin Dressing** (see page 117) or the dressing of your choice.

Sprinkle sesame seeds over the top and serve.

QUINOA SALAD

3 cups quinoa, cooked
  (see page 72)
¼– ½ cup Lime
  Vinaigrette (see page
  116)

¼ cup pine nuts, toasted
1 organic yellow bell
  pepper, diced
6 apricots, dried and
  diced
3 Tbs. organic raisins
  (the golden yellow variety are very pretty in
  this salad)
2 Tbs. currants, dried
1 tsp. salt
2 Tbs. cilantro or chives,
  fresh and chopped

lettuce leaves, rinse and
  dry and leave whole

sprigs of flat-leaf parsley
lime wedges

In a large mixing bowl, toss together the quinoa and lime vinaigrette dressing.

In a separate bowl combine the pine nuts, apricots, raisins, currants, salt and cilantro or chives. Mix completely and add to the quinoa.

Ladle each serving onto a prepared lettuce leaf. Garnish with a sprig of parsley and a wedge of lime.

SERVING SUGGESTION: Quinoa Salad is a nice 'starch' to accompany any grilled fish.

SOUTHWEST BOUNTY
Fresh Corn, Black Beans & Tomato Salad

This recipe comes from a good friend who entertains more than anyone else I know. So tasty is this summer's harvest combination that she gets requests for repeats every year.

Salad:

2 cups corn kernels, fresh

2 cups black beans

2 cups tomatoes, chopped

2 scallions, chopped

2 tsp. jalapeno, minced (optional)

DRESSING:

1 tsp. cumin

¼ cup lime juice, fresh

1-2 Tbs. extra-virgin olive oil

4 Tbs. cilantro, chopped

½ – 1 tsp. salt (optional)

In a large mixing bowl, combine the salad ingredients together and set aside.

In a heavy skillet, heat the cumin for 1 minute, stirring constantly. Remove from heat. Add lime juice and blend. Slowly whisk in the olive oil, blending completely. Add cilantro and salt.

Pour the dressing over the salad ingredients. Toss to coat vegetables and beans completely.

Cover and refrigerate for 1-3 hours before serving.

NOTE: Do not dress the salad more than 3 hours before serving!

FRENCH LENTILS

A special note: French Lentils are very different from Green Lentils; they do not break down when they are cooked, or even overcooked. They are better prepared as described below, rather than used in a soup, as on page 100.

---

1 cup French lentils (look for the small, red variety)
1 bay leaf
3 cups water

Place the lentils and bay leaf in a saucepan with water and bring to a boil. Boil for 5 minutes, reduce heat, and simmer for 20 minutes.

1 onion, finely chopped
1 carrot, finely chopped
1 stalk celery, finely chopped
1 clove garlic, minced
1 plum tomato, peeled and chopped
2 teaspoon mint leaves, crushed and dried

Add the onion, garlic, carrot and celery. Blend together the plum tomato and mint and add to the cooking lentils. Simmer for 20 minutes more, or until the vegetables are cooked to taste.

Juice of ⅓ – ½ lemon

Add the lemon juice and serve.

> "Legumes actually enrich the soil they grow in, while other plants, including the grains, deplete it. ... The seeds of legumes are twice as rich in protein as are grains, and are also well stocked in iron and B vitamins. The practice of using them as rotation crops dates back to Roman times."
> – McGee

KIDNEY BEAN SALAD

This high-protein, high-fiber bean salad makes a wonderful potluck or summer barbecue contribution. You'll quickly gain notoriety and receive repeat requests for this dish. The high-protein, high-fiber also makes this ideal for a detox.

2 cups cooked kidney
beans (see page 59)

1 onion, medium
½ green pepper
½ sweet red pepper
fresh flat parsley
fresh dill
1 bunch scallions
1 Tbs. horse radish

DRESSING:

1 clove garlic, pressed
1 teaspoon mustard
¼ cup rice vinegar
salt
sepper
½ cup peanut oil, organ-
ic and cold pressed

Place drained beans in a mixing bowl.

Finely chop onion, peppers, parsley and dill. Add to the beans. Finely slice the greens ends of the scallions and add to the bean mixture. Stir in horse radish and blend ingredients completely. Make a mustard vinaigrette by pressing garlic clove into a small bowl. Add mustard and mix til paste-like. Add vinegar, salt and pepper, and blend thoroughly. Slowly add the peanut oil, whipping as you go.

Pour the vinaigrette over the bean mixture. Stir so that all of the beans are covered with the dressing. Chill and serve.

MARINARA SAUCE

A reliable basic for tomato lovers.

---

2 Tbs. extra-virgin olive oil
3 cloves garlic, minced

1 onion, large, diced
1 green pepper, diced
1 stalk celery, diced finely

4 cups tomatoes, peeled and diced
1 Tbs. basil
1 tsp. oregano
1 tsp. salt

In a heavy stock pot on a medium temperature, heat the oil. Add the garlic and swirl and stir to flavor the oil but do not let the garlic brown.

Add the onion, green pepper and celery. Stir well so that the vegetables are covered with the garlic and oil. Allow to cook for 10-15 minutes on medium to medium-low heat. Stir occasionally. Onions will appear translucent.

Add the tomatoes, basil, oregano and salt. Continue to cook the marinara over medium heat for 45 minutes.

Serve immediately over **Veggies on the Half-Shell** (see page 84), **Baked Fish** (see page 36), or whatever you desire. Refrigerate leftovers.

BAKED FISH
with Sweet Red Peppers

4 Tbs. extra-virgin olive oil
1 sweet red pepper, diced
5 cloves garlic, minced
¼ teaspoon saffron
cayenne, to taste (optional)

2 lbs. cod, scrod, halibut or sea bass fillet
½ teaspoon thyme
salt
pepper

4 tsp. fresh parsley

Preheat oven to 400 °F.

Dice the sweet red pepper. Heat 2 tablespoons of olive oil in large skillet and add red pepper. Cook until soft. Add garlic, saffron and cayenne. Cook for 30 seconds.

Cut fish into about 8 chunks. Spread vegetable mixture in bottom of casserole dish and add fish in a single layer. Turn fish chunks so that they are coated with the vegetable and oil mixture. Fold under any thin ends of the fish fillet. Drizzle 2 tablespoons olive oil over the fish and sprinkle with crumbled thyme, salt and pepper. Cover with foil and bake for 15 minutes.

Sprinkle minced parsley over fish. Baste with pan juices and serve.

POACHED COD
with Parsley Horseradish Sauce

1 lb cod or scrod

½ cup fresh parsley, finely chopped
1 Tbs. rice vinegar
½ tsp. paprika
1½ Tbs. horseradish
¼ cup extra-virgin olive oil

In a deep, heavy skillet place fish steaks with enough water to cover thm over by 1". Cover the skillet and bring the water to a simmer. Poach fish for 5-6 minutes or until they are flakey. (You can test them for done-ness by gently scraping against the top of the fish with a fork)

While fish is poaching, mix parsley with rice vinegar, paprika and horseradish. Whisk in olive oil.

Transfer fish to plates with a slotted spatula and spoon sauce over them.

BAKED SALMON
with Tarragon and Red Potatoes

6 small red potatoes,
thinly sliced

2 tsp. extra-virgin olive
oil
salt
pepper

1 pound salmon steak
2 Tbs. tarragon, fresh, or
1 tsp. dry tarragon
1 lemon, thinly sliced

Preheat oven to 475°F.
Cook potatoes for no
more than 5 minutes in
boiling water. Drain.

In a large mixing bowl
combine the olive oil,
½ teaspoon of salt and a
dash of black pepper.
Add the potato slices and
toss to coat the potatoes
completely.

Arrange potato slices on a
baking sheet, overlapping
them slightly. Place
salmon in a sheet of either
parchment paper or alu-
minum foil. On top of it,
put the tarragon, ½ tea-
spoon of salt and the
lemon slices. Roll up the
edges and fold and tuck
to create a self-contained
cooking packet. Place the
packet on the baking
sheet alongside potatoes.
Bake until potatoes are
golden brown – about 15
minutes.

Caution:
Be careful when open-
ing the packet! A gush of
steam will need to escape.

SCALLOPS SAUTEED

2 Tbs. oil (grapeseed or peanut)
3 cloves garlic, minced
½ - 1 Tbs. ginger, fresh and minced

1-1½ lbs. scallops (slice in half if they are large)

¼ cup basil, fresh and minced
salt and pepper, to taste

Heat a heavy skillet over medium-high heat. Add oil. Swirl pan. Immediately add the garlic and ginger. Stir several times. The garlic and ginger will flavor the cooking oil but should not brown.

Now add the scallops and stir completely. Keep the scallops tossing and turning! When they are firm and their color has turned from translucent to white, they are finished cooking. Remove from heat. Toss with the fresh basil, season with salt and pepper to taste, and serve.

SERVING SUGGESTION:
For an especially tasty combination that guarantees good eye appeal, too, serve scallops with **Mashed Sweet & White Potatoes** (pg. 70) or **Squash & Potato Puree** (pg. 74) and hearty helping of **Green Beans Almondine** (pg. 66).

SIMPLE SALMON
Baked with Lemon

This version is designed to serve a crowd (8-10) but can easily be modified for a smaller gathering — or dinner for one, if you like! Simply reduce the amount of fish.

---

5 – 6 pound piece of
  salmon
½ teaspoon salt
juice of ½ lemon

lemon wedges
parsley sprigs

Preheat oven to 325°F.

Lay fish on a piece of aluminum foil in a shallow baking pan. Lightly sprinkle all over with salt and lemon juice.

Bake for 1 hour.

Peel off skin – it will come off very easily in a single piece. Serve on a hot platter and garnish with fresh lemon wedges and sprigs of parsley.

SWORDFISH KABOBS

1 pound swordfish or other medium-fat fish fillets

¼ cup fresh lime juice

3 Tbs. extra-virgin olive oil

½ tsp. salt

1 Tbs. cilantro, fresh and chopped

1 cup pineapple chunks

2 small zucchini, cut into chunks

1 sweet red pepper, cut into 1" pieces

Cut fish into bite-sized pieces. Mix lime juice, olive oil, cilantro, salt and garlic in a shallow bowl. Stir to coat fish pieces completely. Cover and refrigerate for at least 30 minutes, but no longer than 2 hours.

Remove fish from marinade and set leftover marinade aside to use later when basting kabobs on the grill. Alternating fish with the fruit and vegetables, thread fish chunks, pineapple, zucchini and peppers onto metal skewers. (Leave a bit of space between pieces to allow everything to cook through.)

Grill kabobs, turning them and brushing them with marinade several times. Fish is ready to eat when it flakes easily with a fork.

SPICY SHRIMP
Kabobs for the Grill

1½ pounds shrimp,
  uncooked and peeled
juice of 1 lemon
1 Tbs. extra-virgin olive
  oil
1 teaspoon cumin
½ teaspoon coriander
pinch of paprika
½ teaspoon salt

2 limes, cut into ½"
  slices

In a shallow bowl combine shrimp with lemon juice, olive oil, and spices. Toss to coat shrimp completely. Cover and refrigerate for about an hour.

Remove shrimp from marinade. Set leftover marinade aside for basting kabobs on the grill.

Quarter each lime slice and thread the kababs onto skewers, alternating shrimp and lime wedges. Leave an air space between pieces to allow the shrimp to cook through.

Grill kabobs for 5-10 minutes, turning and basting several times, until the shrimp are pink and firm.

WHITE BEANS, SHRIMP & SOY PASTA

1 pound soy pasta in a fun, spiral shape

2 cups prepared cannellini beans (refer to page 59)

1 cup chicken broth, organic, preservative-free

1 Tbs. extra-virgin olive oil

2 cloves garlic, minced

¾ pound shrimp, shelled

4 – 5 plum tomatoes, fresh, thinly sliced

2 Tbs. flat-leaf parsley, chopped

½ tsp. salt

pepper to taste

Cook pasta according to package instructions.

In a blender, puree half of the beans and all of the broth. Transfer the beans to a sauce pan and heat, but do not bring to a boil. Set aside.

In a skillet, heat the oil and add the garlic. Swirl to flavor the oil. Add the shrimp and cook until they turn pink. Remove the shrimp and set aside. Add the tomato slices to the skillet and cook for a moment. Return the shrimp to the skillet with the parsley, salt and pepper. Cook over medium heat for just 1 minute. In a separate bowl, toss the cooked pasta with the heated bean puree. Add the shrimp and tomato mixture. Toss completely. Garnish with additional parsley leaves.

FRIED RICE with SEAFOOD

2-3 Tbs. wheat-free soy sauce

1 Tbs. rice vinegar

1 Tbs. water

½ teaspoon pepper

4 scallions, trimmed and sliced

1 Tbs. canola oil

2 cloves garlic, minced

1 Tbs. ginger, fresh and minced

1 onion, small, chopped

1 sweet red pepper, diced

½ pound shrimp, peeled

½ pound scallops (if you're using large Sea Scallops, slice them in half)

4 cups cooked rice (we recommend brown for nutritional value)

In a small bowl, combine the soy sauce, vinegar, water and pepper and set aside.

Heat a Chinese-style wok or other large, heavy skillet. Add oil. When the oil is hot, add the garlic and ginger, swirling to flavor the oil. Then add the whites of the scallions, the onion and red peppers. Saute for 2-3 minutes.

Add seafood and continue to stir fry until shrimp and scallops are cooked through.

Add the rice, stirring entire mixture thoroughly. Add the reserved soy sauce mixture and green scallion ends. Stir and serve.

CLAM SAUCE

1 Tbs. extra-virgin olive
  oil
1 garlic clove, minced
1 onion, large, thinly
  sliced
1 tomato, large, finely
  chopped
10–12 oz. shelled clams
  in their natural juices*

3 leaves fresh basil,
  shredded on the cutting
  board with a knife
½ tsp. oregano, dried
salt
pepper
1 lemon wedge

fresh parsley, chopped

* This is an "eating
clean" replacement for
canned clams. They are
available in the fish
dept. of large supermar-
kets or old-fashioned fish
markets.

Heat the olive oil in a
deep-sided skillet over
medium heat. Add the
garlic and onion and gen-
tly cook, stirring occasionally, until onions are
translucent. Add the tomato, lower heat, and simmer
until you can see that the
tomato is just beginning to
break down. Now, add the
clams.

Add the basil, oregano,
salt and pepper. Squeeze
the juice of the lemon
wedge into the simmering
mixture. Continue cook-
ing on a low heat for a few
minutes but be careful
that the liquid does not
completely evaporate.
Add the parsley; stir and
serve.

SERVING SUGGESTION:
Try serving this over a
baked spaghetti squash,
for the look and feel of
conventional pasta.

BEST OF ALL WORLDS CHILI:
Chunky Chicken & Black Bean Combo

This one-pot meal can provide you with brown-bag lunches for a week or feed a crowd for a weekend get-together.

¾ lb. organic, preservative-free chicken breast meat, cut into 1" chunks

1 Tbs. chili powder

1 tsp. cumin

1 Tbs. extra-virgin olive oil

1 onion, chopped

1 sweet red pepper, diced

3 cloves garlic, minced

½ cup fresh salsa (see page 124)

½ cup organic, pesticide-free chicken broth

2 cups tomatoes, blanched and skinned

1½ cups black beans, cooked

cilantro, minced (optional)

Time-saving option:
After chicken chunks are browned, place all of the ingredients in a crock pot, set it on 'low', and leave it to cook on its own for the day.

Combine chicken and spices in a large bowl. Toss ingredients gently and set aside.

Heat oil in a stock pot over medium-high heat. Add onion. Stir onion so that it is coated with the oil and cook for about 5 minutes or until it begins to have a translucent appearance.

Add the chicken, sweet red pepper and garlic. Cook for another 3 minutes. The outside of the chicken should be slightly golden.

Now add the salsa, chicken broth and tomatoes. Cook for 10 minutes. Stir in the black beans and cook for 10 more minutes.

Serve over brown rice, garnished with a sprinkling of freshly minced cilantro.

CHICKEN AND OKRA STEW
1-pot Meal, South American Style

The first time I tasted "**Frango com Quiabo**", the chicken had been caught that morning and the okra was fresh-picked. The cuisines from around the globe are an inspiration!

2 Tbs. plus 1 Tbs. extra-virgin olive oil

6 cloves garlic, minced
(used 2 cloves at a time)

8 organically raised, pre-servative-free chicken thighs, skinned

1 lb. okra, thinly sliced
2 tsp. white vinegar

4 scallion tops, sliced
2 tsp. salt

DR. THYR'S DETOX TIP:
Okra is known to lubricate the intestines. This lubrication helps relieve constipation, which is important to avoid when doing any kind of detox, and certainly impor-tant for a long and healthy life.

In a large pot, heat oil over medium-high heat. Add 2 cloves of garlic and stir. Aadd chicken thighs (as many as will fit in a single layer). Allow chicken to sizzle and brown on each side. Cook in batches if necessary. Remove chicken. Drain off and discard fat.

In a separate heavy sauce pan, heat 1 Tbs. oil. Add 2 cloves garlic. Stir. Add okra and stir to coat with oil. Cook over medium heat until okra achieves a 'stringy' consistency. Stir in vinegar. Cook for 3 more minutes and then remove from heat.

In the first pan, place 2 cloves garlic, salt and 1½ cups water. Turn heat to medium-high and cook until mixture almost boils. Add chicken, okra and scallion tops and cook over medium-high heat for 20-30 minutes or until okra has cooked down and you have a stew-like consistency.

CHICKEN & CASHEW
SPICEY STIR-FRY

Stir-fries are almost one-pan meals. And they cook up quickly,
too, once the vegetables are prepared.

2 cloves garlic, minced
1 thin slice fresh ginger,
  minced (about the
  diameter of a quarter)
1 Tbs. peanut oil

3 organic, pesticide-free
  boneless, skinless
  chicken breasts, cut in
  2" strips

3 cups broccoli, florets
  and chopped stalks

3 scallions, cut in 3"
  lengths

2 Tbs. wheat-free tamari
  sauce
2 tsp. sesame oil
½ tsp. crushed red pep-
  per flakes

3 Tbs. cashew halves

Heat a wok or heavy skil-
let over high heat. Add
olive oil. Swirl pan and
add garlic and ginger.
Press these into the oil so
that they release their full
flavor. Add the chicken
pieces. Keep heat on high
and stirring constantly,
cook the chicken for 3-5
minutes. Remove chicken
from pan and set aside.

Add broccoli to the pan
and cook over high heat,
stirring and tossing con-
stantly, for 3-5 minutes.
Broccoli will be bright
green; florets will be tender. Return the chicken to
the pan. Add scallions.
Toss and reduce heat to
medium.

In a small bowl combine
tamari sauce, sesame
oil and red pepper flakes.
Pour over the chicken and
broccoli. Stir and continue to cook mixture for
2-3 more minutes. Mix in
the cashews. Remove
from heat and serve
immediately.
Serve over steamed brown
rice.

CHICKEN SATE

Indonesian-style chicken barbecued or broiled on a skewer.

1 Tbs. wheat-free tamari sauce
2 shallots, sliced
1 clove garlic, minced
⅛ tsp. chili powder
1 Tbs. lemon juice, fresh

2 lb. chicken breasts, boneless and skinless, organic and pesticide-free; cut into bite-size cubes

Bamboo skewers, pre-soaked in water for 10 minutes

Mix the tamari, shallots, garlic, chili powder and lemon juice in a large bowl.

Add chicken chunks. Stir so that the chicken is completely covered by the spicy marinade. Cover and chill for 1 hour.

Thread chicken chunks onto skewers, leaving about ¼" space in between each piece.

Barbecue or broil for 5-8 minutes, turning skewers once every minute so that chicken doesn't burn and cooks thoroughly.

Serve immediately. The **Pacific Rim Dipping Sauce** (page 125) is good accompaniment.

CURRIED CHICKEN

The traditional Thai recipe calls for white potato.
I've replaced those with sweet potatoes, a simple carbohydrate
with the added benefit of more fiber content, beta carotene,
iron, potassium, and vitamins B6 and C.

---

1 2½ lb. chicken, organic and preservative-free; skinned and cut into 8 pieces

4 sweet potatoes, peeled and quartered

6 cups coconut milk (page 20)

1 Tbs. curry powder (page 126)

2 tsp. salt

1 tsp. xylitol*

> * Read more about this natural sweetener on page 26.

In a large soup pot place the chicken, potatoes and coconut milk. Simmer for 1 hour uncovered. During this time, the amount of liquid should reduce down to 4 cups. Remove pot from heat and allow to cool. Skim off fat.

In a small saucepan, place 3 Tbs. of the coconut milk from the soup pot. Add curry powder. Mix and heat slowly, stirring often. Add this curry paste to the soup pot, as well as the salt and xylitol.

Over a medium-low heat, reheat the contents of the soup pot.

Serve immediately over a bed of steamed basmati, jasmine or brown rice. Garnish each dish with chopped tomatoes.

INDONESIAN CHICKEN CURRY

The combination of ingredients in this dish deliver a spicier punch than the milder flavors of the Thai Chicken Curry (page 50).

1 chicken, organic and pesticide-free, cut into quarters

1 Tbs. lemon juice, fresh
1 Tbs. oil, extra-virgin olive or canola
1 Tbs. tamari sauce
¼ tsp. salt
1 tsp. chili powder
¼ cup peanut butter, unsweetened
1 Tbs. onion, diced
1 clove garlic, minced
1 Tbs. curry powder (page 126)

"Curries are a wonderful warming food to eat on a detox and in general. The curry spices are often very good for liver function too, especially the turmeric."—Dr. Thyr

Arrange chicken in a single layer in a glass baking dish.

Mix together all of the other ingredients and pour the mixture over the chicken pieces. Cover and refrigerate for 6-8 hours.

An hour-and-a-half before serving time, preheat your oven to 350°F.

Remove chicken dish from refrigerator. Discard cover and bake for 30 minutes. Remove from oven. Baste chicken with pan juices. Cover dish with a sheet of aluminum foil and return pan to the oven for another hour. Remove from oven. Serve over brown rice.

MEDITERRANEAN CHICKEN
with CHICKPEAS

1 lb. organic, pesticide-free chicken, boneless, skinless breasts, sliced in 1"–wide strips
salt
1 Tbs. extra-virgin olive oil

1 medium-sized onion, sliced
½ green pepper
½ sweet red pepper
2 cloves garlic, minced

2 cups prepared chick peas
2 tomatoes, peeled and diced
1 Tbs. basil
1 tsp oregano
salt to taste

Lightly sprinkle salt on chicken pieces. Heat olive oil in a wok or deep skillet on medium-high heat. Add chicken and cook until brown on both sides.

Add onions, peppers and garlic. Stir well and continue to cook.

Lower the heat slightly. Add chick peas, tomatoes and herbs. Cover and simmer for about 10 minutes, until chicken is thoroughly cooked.

Serve over brown rice or a baked potato.

SALAD NIÇOISE

The proportions and exact ingredients vary from café to café. However, tuna, tomatoes, onion, lettuce, and a homemade olive oil-vinaigrette dressing are the standard. Anchovies are the other French 'must'. The canned variety available here doesn't comply with a pure eating clean philosophy; we leave that choice to your own discretion.

A NOTE ABOUT the INGREDIENTS:
Amounts indicated below are for a 1-person salad. If you are preparing a large, family-style salad platter, increase ingredient quantities accordingly.

- 4 oz. tuna, grilled or baked
- 1 cup mixed salad greens, rinsed and dried
- ½ cup Green beans, steamed
- ½ tomatoes, cut in wedges
- 1 egg, hard-boiled
- 3 – 5 black olives (in lieu of the Frenchest of French ingredients, the Niçoise olive, I suggest Kalamari Greek olives)
- ¼ green pepper, thinly sliced
- 1 Tbs. sweet white onion, diced or 1 scallion, sliced
- 2 Tbs. Basic Vinaigrette Dressing (page 115)

Create a family-style Salad Niçoise on a large platter or assemble individual salad plates and serve each person separately. On the bed of salad greens, with the exception of the onion or scallion, arrange groupings of each ingredient, working your way around the plate. Gently scatter the onion or scallion across the entire salad. Complete individual salad plates with 2 Tbs. dressing each. Vinaigrette dressing quantity for a large platter will vary on size and taste.

GREEK BEEF STEW

This family favorite was passed down to my father from his Uncle Costa, a Greek sea captain known for his passion for preparing wholesome meals. Notice how the onions offset the tart vinegar, yet both flavors remain in balance.

---

30 pearl onions

1½ lbs. organically raised, preservative-free beef: steak tips

¾ cup red wine vinegar

¼ cup extra-virgin olive oil

1 tomato, diced

1 Tbs. pickling spice (available in the spice section of the grocery)

cheese cloth, 6″ square

Blanch the pearl onions and squeeze the skins off them. Cover the bottom of an 8-9″ heavy, lidded pot with the onions. Cut the steak tips into 1″ lengths to approximate cubes and place the cubes on top of the onions so that the onions are covered.

Mix red wine vinegar, olive oil and tomato and pour over the meat.

Make up a tablespoon of pickling spices in a gauze bag and push it down amongst the pieces of meat.

Cover and simmer for 1½ hours with the lid tightly closed.

Garnish with chopped parsley. Serve in soup bowls with 2-3 table-spoons of liquid in each.

A WORD ABOUT BEEF:
"Organic is absolutely crucial when buying beef! Beef is not a good fat, even if it is organic, and should be eaten sparingly."
— Dr. Sara Thyr

TURKEY & AVOCADO SANDWICH

2 slices rice or spelt
  bread, toasted
¼ avocado, sliced
2 ounces free-range, pre-
  servative-free sliced
  turkey breast
1 lettuce leaf
2 tomato slices
1 onion slice (optional)

Layer lettuce, tomato, onion, avocado and turkey onto one slice of the bread. Top with the other slice of bread and ... there's lunch!

CLEAN SOLUTION: Do you miss the creamy quality of mayonnaise? Consider using avocado slices that are soft enough to spread on the bread. Makes a satisfying mayo replacement!

Vegetables,
Beans
and Rice

BEANS

Make-ahead kidney, chick pea, pinto or black beans

It's good practice to rinse dried beans before preparing them, and to finger through them looking for unwelcome small stones and twigs.

To pre-soak or not to pre-soak? Authorities are divided on this and the nutritional benefits to be gained or lost. Whether you boil, pressure-cook, or slow-cook your beans in a crock pot, they will achieve the necessary degree of doneness regardless of pre-soaking. No matter what you decide, pre-soaking will reduce cooking time. Pre-soaking and rinsing can also decrease their flatulence effect. Cook the beans with kombo seaweed (a 2–4" piece) for additional help in reducing their flatulent effect.

TO BOIL BEANS: Place beans in a large pot. Add enough cold water to cover by 2". Over a high heat, bring contents to a boil. Reduce the heat to low. Cover and simmer, stirring occasionally until beans are tender. Replenish water as needed.
Cooking time will vary with type of bean.

PRESSURE-COOKING BEANS: This is the fastest method for cooking beans. Refer to your user manual for specific bean-to-water guidelines. In addition, it is recommended to add 1 Tbs. oil per cup of beans to prevent frothing.

SLOW COOKING IN THE CROCK POT: Place beans in crock pot and cover with 3-4" water. Set on high and allow to cook for 5-8 hours. Times vary.

CHICK PEAS

1½ cups dry chick peas
water

In a large bowl, soak the chick peas in a generous amount of water for 2-3 hours. Drain and rinse the beans. Transfer them to a large sauce pan. Add enough water to cover more than 2" and boil for 1½ hours or until chick peas are very soft. I recommend that you check on the pot every 20 minutes or so. If the water is boiling down quickly, add extra water to the pot so that the chick peas are always more than just covered with water.

Once the chick peas have been boiled to a soft, mashable state, they are ready to eat, as-is, in a salad. Or, follow the recipe for HUMUS on page 123 and turn these protein-packed nuggets into an irresistible sandwich spread or dip.

> "The chick pea was known in Rome as **cicer arietinum**: the second word means ramlike (the first names the legume itself), and refers to the seed's resemblance to a ram's head, complete with curling horns."
> – McGee

PINTO BEANS

The essence of this dish is the balance of the sweetness of the onion against the tart flavor of the lemon. Better to use a large onion than a small one. Taste the dish before serving to get the right amount of lemon.

1 Vidalia onion, finely chopped

1-2 garlic cloves, thinly sliced

1 Tbs. extra-virgin olive oil

1½ cups cooked pinto beans (see page 59)

2 Tbs. tomato, crushed or finely chopped

1-2 tsp. dried mint

freshly ground pepper to taste

juice of ⅓ - ½ lemon

Garlic and onions are wonderful on a detox for their sulfur addition.

Vidalia onions have a unique sweetness. However, if they are not available at your market, any large white onion will suffice. Finely chop the onion. Heat the olive oil in a sauce pan. Add the sliced garlic. Swirl and stir garlic in the oil; this flavors the oil and enhances the overall flavor of the dish. Then add the onion, cover the pot and saute until the onion is transparent but not brown.

Add the beans and liquid, the chopped or crushed tomato, mint and pepper. Simmer for 15 minutes.

Add the lemon, stir and serve.

ACORN SQUASH ON THE HALF-SHELL

2 acorn squash, rinsed and sliced lengthwise; discard seeds

1 Tbs. peanut oil
2 apples, Cortland or Golden Delicious (or other good 'cooking' apple), peeled and diced
½ cup onion, chopped
¼ cup raisins
1 tsp. cinnamon

1 Tbsp. molasses

Preheat oven to 350 °F.

Heat a heavy skillet over medium heat. Add oil and swirl the pan to warm the oil. Then add the apples, onion, raisins and cinnamon. Cook until onion looks translucent.

Stir in molasses.

Set acorn halves in a glass baking dish. Add enough water to fill pan ½". Stuff the cavities of the 4 acorn halves with the apple-onion mixture. Bake for 30 minutes or until squash is tender when pierced with a fork.

Remove from oven and serve immediately.

ARTICHOKES DIVINE

Artichokes are a particularly liver-friendly food. When Dr. Thyr recommended that I include them in my diet during my detox, it was like a gift. But then I realized the challenge: how to love them without the butter! Try this roasted variation.

5 artichokes, medium-
sized
1 lemon, sliced in half

2 Tbs. lemon juice, fresh
2 tsp. salt

3 Tbs. extra-virgin olive
oil
1 clove garlic, minced
½ tsp. salt
1 pinch black pepper

Preheat oven to 400 °F. Trim the bottom off each stem. Cut the artichokes in quarters and remove the choke (the 'hairy' center). Rub the exposed interior surfaces of the artichokes with the lemon.

Meanwhile, in a large stock pot, bring 12 cups water to boil with lemon juice and salt. Add the artichokes and allow them to boil until tender (about 5 minutes).

Drain the artichokes. Pat dry. Slice each quarter in half. Place in glass baking dish.

Mix together olive oil, garlic, salt and pepper. Pour mixture over the artichokes and toss to cover.

Bake for 30 minutes, stirring and turning pieces every 5-7 minutes.

Serve hot or at room temperature. If your diet allows, serve with **Pacific Rim Dipping Sauce** (see page 125).

BAKED STRING BEANS

2 Tbs. extra-virgin olive oil

2 cloves garlic, thinly sliced or minced

1 Spanish onion, thinly sliced

½ carrot, grated

1½ cup tomatoes, chopped

Preheat oven to 250 °F. In a sauce pan or skillet, heat olive oil. Add garlic, onion and grated carrot. Stir and then add chopped tomatoes. Simmer until everything breaks down and blends together.

1 tsp. oregano

2 Tbs. fresh parsley

2 Tbs. mint, fresh or dried

2 tomatoes, pureed in the blender

pepper

Add in the oregano, chopped parsley, mint, pureed tomato and black pepper to taste. Stir and simmer for a few minutes.

1 lb. string beans, fresh

Rinse beans. Remove the ends but leave the rest whole. Add them to the tomato mixture. Cover and bake in the oven for 2½ hours.

GREEN BEAN SALAD

1½ pounds green beans, fresh

½ cup extra-virgin olive oil

¼ cup rice vinegar

2 cloves garlic, minced

½ tsp. salt

¾ cup Bermuda onion, finely diced

Rinse green beans and trim off ends, leaving the beans whole. Steam them until they are tender but still firm (5-8 minutes).

Meanwhile, prepare the marinade. Blend pressed garlic with the olive oil. Add the salt and a dash of pepper. As you add the rice vinegar, maintain a whisking motion with a fork.

In a large bowl, while the beans are still hot, toss them with the marinade. Allow to cool.

Add onion and mix. Cover and refrigerate for several hours before serving.

GREEN BEANS ALMONDINE

1 lb. fresh green string beans

1 Tbs. peanut oil
2 cloves garlic, minced

⅓ cup raw almonds, chopped or slivered
salt, to taste

Rinse and trim the green beans, leaving their lengths whole. In a large lidded pot outfitted with a steamer, steam beans until tender – about 7 or 8 minutes. Remove from heat and set aside.

Heat a wok or large heavy skillet. Add oil and garlic and swirl the pan several times before adding steamed beans, so that the garlic cooks just slightly. Keep heat high and toss and stir the beans constantly for 1 minute.

Add almonds and salt to taste. Toss and serve immediately.

VARIATION: Use a combination of both green and yellow wax string beans. Still delicious and even more colorful!

BEET SALAD

Beets are highly recommended for those doing a liver detoxification diet or if you're looking for foods that specifically support liver function.

1 lb. beets, scrubbed clean with skins left intact; cut off leaves, leaving 1–2" stem

Vidalia onion, sliced thin

¼ cup rice vinegar
2 tsp. extra-virgin olive oil

In a large stock pot, bring 12 cups of water to boil. Add 1½ teaspoons salt. Add beets and allow water to come back to a boil. Cover and cook until beets are tender and can be pierced with a fork (30-35 minutes for medium-sized beets; 45-60 minutes for larger ones).

Drain beets in a colander. Rinse with cold water. When they are cool enough to handle, peel off skins, remove leaf stems and root threads. Thinly slice (⅛-¼" thick) into a mixing bowl. Add onions.

In a separate bowl, blend rice vinegar and olive oil. Pour dressing over beets and onions. Toss thoroughly so that vegetables are completely covered by dressing.

Cover and refrigerate for 2 hours before serving.

EGGPLANT CAVIAR

This recipe is another tasty souvenir I brought back from
the south of France!

3 eggplant, cut in half
and 'scored' on the cut
surface

3-4 shallots, finely diced
3 garlic cloves, minced
extra-virgin olive oil
1 pastry brush

Cumin (optional)
Coriander (optional)
Sage (optional)

Preheat oven to 350°F.

Brush surface of egg-plants with the olive oil and sprinkle with salt and pepper. Set eggplants on a cookie sheet and bake in preheated oven for 30 minutes.

Pour olive oil in heavy skillet. Heat and add shallots and garlic. Saute til golden and glistening.

Remove eggplant from the oven. Scrape out the meat into a large mixing bowl. Discard skins. Mash up the eggplant meat with a fork or potato masher. Add shallots and garlic. Salt and pepper to taste. Optional seasonings such as cumin, coriander or sage will lend a decidedly Mediterranean flavor to your Eggplant Caviar. Serve as a dip.

EGGPLANT FRITTERS

Eggplant lovers rejoice. There's no end to the possibilities!

---

1 eggplant, large

1 clove garlic, minced

2 Tbs. flat-leaf parsley, chopped

½ cup rice, cooked and pureed in a blender or finely chopped

1 egg, beaten

¼ tsp. cumin

¼ tsp. coriander

¾ tsp. sea salt

¼ tsp. pepper

peanut or canola oil

SERVING SUGGESTION:
Place a patty or two on a bed of lettuce or on the side as a 'meaty' addition to a garden salad.
Dress with **Basic Vinaigrette** (page 115) or **More Tahini Dressing** (page 119).

Preheat oven to 425°F. Rinse off and pat dry the eggplant. Place it on a lightly oiled baking sheet and bake for 30-45 minutes or until tender. Remove from oven and cool until comfortable to handle. Slice in half. Scoop out the meat of the eggplant into a mixing bowl. With a fork or potato masher, work the meat into a puree consistency. Add the garlic, parsley, rice, egg and spices. Mix well. Shape into patties, using about ½-cup for each.

Heat 2 Tbs. oil in a heavy skillet over medium heat. When the oil is hot, add patties and cook until they are golden brown. This should take about 2 minutes for each side. Drain and cool on paper towels. Serve hot or at room temperature.

MASHED POTATOES
Sweet & White

3 white potatoes, peeled and cut into 2" chunks
3 sweet potatoes, peeled and cut into 2" chunks

1 clove garlic, minced
1–2 cups chicken organic, preservative-free
salt and pepper to taste
2–3 Tbs. parsley, chopped

Put potato chunks into a large stock pot. Cover with cold water, filling the pot enough to leave 2" or more above the potatoes. Bring to a boil. Lower heat to medium-high and continue to gently boil potatoes until they are tender (but not mushy!) and can be pierced easily with a fork.

Drain. Return cooked potato to the pot. Starting with 1 cup of broth added to the potatoes, begin to mash by hand with a potato masher. When you've added enough broth to achieve the desired mashed potato consistency, season to taste with the minced garlic, salt, pepper and parsley.

Don't forget to garnish each serving with an extra sprinkle of parsley!

POPEYE SPECIAL:
Sauteed Leafy Greens

The healthful benefits of eating leafy green vegetables on a regular basis have been the constant refrain of nutritionists and mothers for years. Here's an appetizing solution.

---

1 Tbs. extra-virgin olive oil

3 cloves garlic, minced

1 cup mushrooms, sliced

8 cups leafy green vegetables (spinach, collard greens, red chard — a mixture of two or three or choose just one); rinsed, stems removed, leaves chopped

Heat oil in a large, deep skillet or a heavy lidded sauce pan. Add garlic and stir to flavor the oil.

Toss in the mushrooms and stir to coat completely with garlic and oil.

Add leafy greens and 1 Tbs. water. Cover. Reduce heat to low. Allow to simmer 3-5 minutes or until greens are tender.

SERVING SUGGESTION: A great accompaniment to broiled fish.

QUINOA
with Saffron & Spinach

A Dr. Sara Thyr favorite! QUINOA (pronounced: KEEN-wah) is an ancient grain high in protein and B & E vitamins. Look for it in larger supermarkets or your favorite health food store.

1½ cups quinoa

2 cups + 1 Tbs. water
1 Tbs. extra-virgin olive oil
¼ tsp. + a sprinkling salt
⅛ tsp. saffron threads, crushed

1 lb. spinach, fresh, rinsed
2 cloves garlic, minced
wheat-free tamari or soy sauce (optional)

In a mixing bowl, cover quinoa with water. Gently rub the grains between the palms of your hands. Drain and rinse until water runs clear.

In a lidded sauce pan, bring the 2 cups water to a boil. Add ½ Tbs. extra-virgin olive oil, salt, saffron and quinoa. Reduce heat to low and simmer for 20-25 minutes. Quinoa grains should have a translucent appearance and be tender but not mushy. Remove from heat, cover pot and set aside.

In a large soup pot, heat oil. Add garlic and swirl the pot to flavor the oil. Add the spinach, 1 Tbs. water, a sprinkling of salt, and reduce heat. Cover and simmer for 3-5 minutes.

To serve, scoop a cup of quinoa onto each plate; top with some spinach.

RATATOUILLE

This was served as an accompaniment to broiled salmon one evening during a cycling tour of the South of France. Bon appetite!

2 eggplant, diced
2 tsp. salt

2 large zucchini, diced
2 onions, diced
2 red peppers (peeled while raw)
4 cloves garlic, minced
4 Tbs. extra-virgin olive oil

1-2 Tbs. Tapenade (see page 120).

Put diced eggplant in a colander and set it over a large bowl or in the sink. Salt eggplant lightly, turning the chunks as you go, so that the meaty surfaces are covered. Allow eggplant to rest for 20 minutes. (The salt will draw out any the bitterness in the eggplant and prepares it for cooking.)

Heat 1 Tbs. olive oil in a heavy sauce pan or skillet. Add garlic and zucchini, toss and stir so that the zucchini chunks are coated with hot oil. Saute until browned. Place cooked zucchini in a colander set in the sink or over a large bowl.

Repeat sauté process with the onions, red peppers and eggplant.

Place all of the cooked vegetables in a large serving bowl. Toss with the Tapenade and serve.

SQUASH and POTATO PUREE

1 butternut squash,
  medium
  extra-virgin olive oil
2 cloves garlic, whole

2 lbs. Russet potatoes,
  peeled and cut into 2"
  chunks

1 cup rice milk
salt and pepper, to taste

Preheat oven to 375°F. Cut the squash lengthwise. Remove and discard seeds. Brush the flesh of the squash with olive oil and lay face down on a cookie sheet. Bake until you can pierce the skin of the squash easily.

While the squash is baking, place potatoes in a large pot and cover with cold water. Bring the water to a boil and continue to cook the potatoes until they are soft (but not mushy). Drain and place potatoes in a large bowl.

When squash is cool enough to handle, scrape the meat of the squash halves into the bowl with the potatoes. Add the garlic. Using a potato masher, begin to blend the squash and potatoes.

Add the rice milk until you achieve a nice, mashed potatoe-like consistency. Season with salt and pepper to taste.

SWEET PEPPER SALAD

Roasting the peppers beforehand may seem like a bit of a nuisance, but the end results will make it worthwhile. It's a promise.

3-4 sweet peppers: red, yellow and green

3 Tbs. extra-virgin olive oil
1 Tbs. tarragon vinegar
OR
1 Tbs. lemon juice, fresh
2-3 Tbs. thyme or basil, fresh and roughly chopped
salt and pepper to taste
⅓ cup black olives

Roast the peppers over your grill or in the oven, keeping close watch and rotating them to prevent scorching. Then, set the peppers aside to cool until they can be handled without burning your fingertips.

Once cooled, peel off and discard the pepper skins; remove and discard the seeds and stems.

Cut peppers lengthwise into thin strips. Place in a shallow serving dish and add the vinegar or lemon juice, thyme or basil, and a pinch of salt and pepper. Toss. Cover and leave peppers to rest in the dressing at room temperature for 1-2 hours before serving.

Garnish with black olives.

FANCY RICE

FOR SPECIAL OCCASIONS OR JUST BECAUSE ...

Fans of sesame flavor will applaud this simple variation.

2 cups chicken broth, organic and preservative-free

1 tsp. sesame oil

1 cup rice (brown, white or basmati)

2 Tbs. toasted sesame seeds

In a lidded sauce pan, bring the broth and sesame oil to a boil.

Stir rice into the boiling broth. Reduce heat to low. Cover and simmer for 20-30 minutes (exact time will depend on the type of rice you use).

Stir in the sesame seeds. Serve.

SWEET RED PEPPERS
and Pasta

A super simple pasta dish using only organic red peppers, garlic and olive oil.

---

2 sweet red peppers, skinned and deseeded
2 cloves garlic, finely chopped
2 Tbs. extra-virgin olive oil

4 oz. soy pasta
2 Tbs. parsley, finely chopped

Drop the peppers into boiling water for a few moments. Remove and allow to drain and cool in a colander. When you can handle them without burning your fingertips, peel off the skins, remove the cores and seeds, and slice into ½"-wide strips.

Heat 1 Tbs. olive oil in a skillet and add 1 clove garlic. Carefully sauté, being careful that garlic doesn't brown. Add the sliced peppers and continue to cook until the garlic is slightly cooked and the peppers warm. Remove the pan from the heat and set aside.

Cook the pasta and drain. In large mixing bowl, mix the remaining olive oil with the other clove of garlic, finely chopped, with the pasta. Place on dinner plates. Add the sliced peppers on top. Garnish with chopped parsley.

REFRIED BEANS

1 Tbs. cold-pressed
canola oil
2–3 cloves garlic,
minced

2 cups pink or pinto
beans, cooked
½–¾ cup water
¼ tsp. salt

Heat oil in heavy-bottomed saucepan. Add garlic and swirl minced pieces around to flavor the oil, but don't let the garlic go brown.

Add beans and enough water to just cover them. If you add too much, don't worry. By allowing the beans to boil down a bit you can achieve the desired thickness. Conversely, if the beans are too thick to be pleasing, simply add water, a little bit at a time, until you are satisfied with the density of the mixture.

Add your salt. A word of caution: it is very easy to over-salt beans. Better to start with a small amount (no more than ¼ tsp. per 2 cups of beans) and add more as taste requires!

SUMMER SALAD
Cucumber, Dill & Red Onion
Remarkably refreshing. Perfect for a hot day.

1 red onion, sliced very
thin

2 cucumbers, peeled
and sliced paper-thin
(seed them, too, if you
prefer)

3 Tbs. rice vinegar

sea salt, to taste

pepper, to taste

¼ cup dill, fresh

In mixing bowl, combine
the onion and cucumbers.
Add rice vinegar, salt and
pepper. Toss well.

Cover and refrigerate 30-
60 minutes.

Remove from refrigerator
and transfer salad to a
serving dish. Sprinkle the
top with the dill. Ready to
serve.

SPANISH RICE WITH BLACK BEANS

1–2 Tbs. extra-virgin olive oil

2 cloves garlic, minced

1 medium-sized onion

½ green pepper, diced

½ sweet red pepper, diced

2 cups cooked rice (brown or white)

¾ cups black beans, cooked and rinsed

2 tsp. cumin

½ tsp. turmeric

½ tsp. saffron

salt and pepper to taste

OPTIONAL:

1 tomato, fresh and diced

1 chicken breast, cooked and diced

Heat oil in a wok or large frying pan with deep sides. When the oil is hot, add garlic and stir to flavor the oil. Then toss in the onion and peppers. Stir and mix so that they are coated in the oil and continue to sauté until they become translucent.

Add rice and beans; stir to mix completely. Add seasonings and continue to heat until mixture is piping hot. Ready to serve.

> Turmeric is a great herb for helping liver function, and can also prevent conversion of carcinogens to cancer.

MOROCCAN SALAD

A refreshing alternative to the standard lettuce-and-tomato fare, introduced to me by my brother-in-law. So delicious, this is on my 'special request list' when I go to his house for dinner.

1 sweet red pepper, roasted whole (see page 86), diced

1 green pepper, roasted whole (see page 86), diced

1 cup parsley, minced

1 cucumber, peeled, seeded, diced

1 tomato, finely chopped

½ onion, medium-sized, chopped fine or shredded

1 small or ½ large head romaine lettuce, shredded

DRESSING:

2–4 Tbs. rice vinegar

2–4 Tbs. extra-virgin olive oil

salt to taste

Basically, all of the ingredients are finely diced before assembling into a large mixing bowl.

In a small bowl, mix equal amounts of the rice vinegar and olive oil together.

Just before serving salad, add dressing, beginning with a small amount. Vegetables should be moistened with the dressing but not swimming in it. Exact dressing amount is up to the discretion of the cook. Serve directly from the mixing bowl or line a large platter with whole lettuce leaves and mound the Moroccan Salad on top.

STIR-FRY VEGETABLES

There is no hard-and-fast rule about what should or should not go into a stir-fry. Ingredients can be determined by what is in season at the market or what you have sitting in your refrigerator. A recipe is simply a launching pad for your own creativity.

1 Tbs. extra-virgin olive oil
2 cloves garlic, minced
2 thin slices ginger root, peeled and minced

½ onion, diced or sliced
3 stalks bok choy cabbage, sliced
1 cup broccoli, flowerettes and chopped stalk
¼ sweet red pepper, sliced
1 cup cauliflower, flowerettes and chopped stalk

1 Tbs. wheat-free tamari or soy sauce
1 Tbs. toasted sesame seeds
½ tsp. sesame oil

Heat a wok or heavy skillet over high heat. Add oil. Swirl the pan and add the garlic and ginger. Stir and swirl so that the garlic and ginger flavor the oil.

Keep heat on high and add the vegetables. Toss and turn the vegetables constantly for about 5 minutes. Broccoli will turn a bright green when it is reaching readiness.

Add tamari, sesame seeds and sesame oil. Mix completely. Remove from heat and serve immediately over brown rice or quinoa.

OPTION: For softer rather than crispy vegetables, add ½ cup chicken or vegetable stock with the tamari. Cover wok or skillet and reduce heat to low. Allow to simmer for 5 minutes, then serve.

VEGGIE MEDLEY PLATTER

A colorful array of fresh vegetables is a feast for the eyes and appetite!

FRESH ORGANIC VEGETABLES:

Ruby or Leaf Lettuce
Carrots
Scallions
Sweet Red Pepper
Green Pepper
Celery
Green Beans
Yellow Wax Beans
Cauliflower
Broccoli
Tomatoes – Cherry or Grape tomatoes are the perfect finger food and will work very well

VEGETABLE DIP:

Choose one, or include a small dish of each:
Humus (page 123) or **Eggplant Caviar** (page 68).

> Set a brightly colored vegetable (carrot) next to a lighter colored vegetable (cauliflower) so that color and type are staggered. Fresh vegetables, especially those in season, are inherently beautiful. Your platter is no exception!

Rinse and dry whole leaves of the lettuce. Arrange in a swirling pattern on a large platter. Fill a small glass bowl with the dip of your choice and set it in the center of the platter. Wash and dry all of the vegetables you are going to include in your platter.
• Carrots – Peel. Remove ends. Make ⅛"-thick slices.
• Broccoli & Cauliflower – Cut into bite-sized flowerlets that are easy to pick up.
• Peppers – Remove center core and make length-wise slices about ¼–½" wide.
• Celery – Remove ends. Divide each stalk into 3" lengths.
• Beans – Remove ends and leave whole.
• Tomatoes – Cherry and Grape tomatoes can be served as-is.
Work from the center of the platter and place fist-sized mounds of each vegetable on the lettuce bed.

VEGGIES ON THE HALF-SHELL

Visiting agricultural areas of the world reminds me how far removed us city-dwellers are from the earth in which our food is cultivated. These were served as an appetizer in the south of France, where open market days are commonplace and variations on tomato, garlic, olive oil and eggplant are daily fare.

2 medium-sized zucchini

2 sweet red pepper

1 medium-sized
eggplant

1–2 tomatoes, skinned +
chopped

2 Tbs. extra-virgin olive
oil

1–2 Tbs. basil

3 cloves garlic, minced

Preheat oven to 350°F.
In a large soup pot of boiling water, blanch* each of the vegetables. When they are cool enough to handle, slice them in half and scoop out their meat, mixing all of the vegetables' innards together in a large mixing bowl. Set empty vegetable halves to the side for later. Add the tomato, olive oil, basil (to taste) and garlic. In batches, puree mixture in a food processor.

Fill the empty vegetable halves with this mixture and heat filled veggie shells in the oven for 15 minutes.

Serve as an appetizer or as a vegetable with your main course.

*to blanch: immerse in boiling water until skins begin to 'wrinkle'.

VEGGIE FRITTATA

A quick and easy breakfast or a hearty meal anytime of the day.
Good for using up leftover steamed vegetables.
This recipe serves 1 — simply increase the egg and vegetables for
more servings.

1 tsp. extra-virgin olive oil

1 Tbs. onion, minced

¼ cup mushrooms, sliced

½ cup of any of the following steamed or sautéed vegetables:
• spinach, chard or kale
• broccoli
• cauliflower
• sweet red and/or green peppers

1–2 eggs, beaten

1 tsp. wheat-free tamari or soy sauce, or amount to taste

Heat a small, heavy skillet. Keep heat on medium-high and add the olive oil. Swirl the pan and add the onions mushrooms. Stir. Cook for 2-3 minutes.

Toss in one or a combination of the vegetables suggested on the left. Stir and cook for another minute.

Pour the beaten egg over the vegetables. Reduce heat to medium-low and allow frittata to cook another 2-3 minutes.

With a spatula, lift the frittata and carefully flip it (like a pancake). Drizzle the tamari over the top of the frittata. Remove from heat and serve.

SERVING SUGGESTION: Serve with a spoonful of steamed brown rice or quinoa.

EASY ROASTED VEGETABLES

to make on the Oven or Grill

A variety works well:
- Green Peppers, cored and cut into 2" chunks or wide strips
- Sweet Red Peppers, cored and cut into 2" chunks or wide strips
- Onions, red or white, peeled and cut into chunks
- Eggplant, ¼–½" wide slices; the new varieties of miniature eggplants are also an excellent choice
- Mushrooms, whole or halved
- Asparagus, thoroughly rinsed and trimmed

extra-virgin olive oil
salt

Preheat oven to 400°F or warm up your outdoor grill. In a large mixing bowl, drizzle a small amount of olive oil over the vegetables. Toss and turn them until they are completely coated in oil. Sprinkle with salt. Toss again.

To roast in the oven, arrange vegetables in a single layer on a cookie sheet. Bake for 5-10 minutes, checking for color. When the tops are brown and sizzling, turn the pieces. Roast for another 5-10 minutes.
Note: Some vegetables cook faster than others. This is to be expected. Simply start stacking finished pieces on a platter and continue roasting the rest until all are done.

To grill, lay each vegetable piece directly on the grill and turn them every couple of minutes, keeping a close eye on them to prevent burning.

SOUP

CHICKEN BROTH

When time and advance planning allow, I find using homemade broth very satisfying. There's a special sense of accomplishment in the knowledge that I prepared a meal so completely. As I said, when time allows ... brew up some stock, store it in 2-cup batches in the freezer, and be happy when you need travel no further than your own kitchen when a recipe calls for it!

1 3 – 4 lb. chicken, organic, preservative-free

12 cups cold water

1 onion, diced
1 carrot, diced
1 celery stalk, diced

1 large square cheesecloth

Remove chicken innards and discard. Place chicken and water in a large stock pot. Bring to a boil. Reduce heat and simmer gently. Keep an eye on the pot and skim off the top any 'scum' that bubbles to the surface. Add vegetables to the soup pot and continue to simmer for about 40 minutes, or until chicken is thoroughly cooked.

Remove from heat. Transfer chicken to a platter and set aside. Strain the broth and vegetable mixture through the cheesecloth into another large container and allow the broth to cool. Once cooled, divide broth into zip-lock freezer bags and freeze these for another day.

Pick the chicken meat off the bones for use in a soup, stir-fry or casserole.

Kitchen Garden in a Pot: Vegetable Soup

1 Tbs. extra-virgin olive oil

1 medium onion, diced

2–3 carrots, sliced

2 stalks celery, chopped

2–3 cloves garlic, minced

1½–2 cups green cabbage, shredded (NOT Bok Choy)

1 cup green beans, fresh or frozen

4–6 fresh tomatoes, peeled and chopped

6 cups organic, preservative-free chicken broth

1 Tbs. basil, fresh or dried

1 tsp. oregano, fresh or dried

salt & pepper, to taste

DRESS-UP OPTIONS:

- Shrimp, previously cooked
- Chicken meat, previously cooked and chopped
- Chick peas

Heat oil over medium-high heat. Add garlic and swirl to flavor the oil. Before garlic turns brown, add the chopped vegetables, stir and cover. Cook on medium to medium-low heat for 5-10 minutes or until onions and celery have softened and are translucent.

Add cabbage, green beans, tomatoes, broth and seasonings. Cover. Reduce heat to low and allow to simmer for at least 30 minutes. Cooking longer will not harm your soup at all but allows the flavors to continue to marry and ripen. Ready to serve.

Any of the DRESS-UP OPTIONS suggested at left will give the soup an extra protein boost.

CURRIED SQUASH SOUP

Guaranteed to warm your bones on a damp and chilly day!

1–2 Tbs. extra-virgin olive oil
1 large onion, diced
3 stalks celery, chopped
3 cloves garlic, pressed

1 Tbs. curry powder (page 126)
1 butternut squash, medium size, peeled and chopped into 1–2" cubes
6 cups organic chicken broth or your favorite vegetable broth
salt & pepper, to taste

Plain yogurt, if not limiting dairy
Chives, minced (optional)

Heat oil in large soup pot. Add onion, celery and garlic and sauté on medium heat until vegetables are soft and translucent.

Sprinkle curry powder over onion and celery, stirring well to coat. Add squash and broth. Turn up the heat and bring mixture to a boil. Then, reduce heat and simmer until squash is soft and easy to pierce with a fork. Taste your broth and season with salt and/or pepper as you like.

Scoop mixture into a blender, pureeing 2-3 cups at a time. Ladle into serving bowls. Garnish each with a dollop of yogurt and a sprinkling of the chopped chives. Serve.

SPICY CARROT SOUP

If you love the idea of a carrot soup, but are not a fan of hot and spicy food, simply eliminate the dried chili pepper and use a bit less of the ginger and curry. Experiment with different types of curry and create your own version !

2 lbs. carrots
5 cups chicken broth, organic, preservative-free
1 dried hot chili pepper
4 tsp. ginger, fresh and minced
3 cloves garlic, pressed
1 tsp. curry (page 126)
1 tsp. cumin
dash of pepper

Peel the carrots and chop them into 1" lengths. Combine all ingredients in a large soup pot. Bring mixture to a boil and then reduce heat and simmer until the carrots are tender and cooked through. Working in batches, puree 2-3 cups of the mixture at a time in a food processor. Return the puree to the soup pot and reheat. Serve.

A WORD FROM DR. THYR
"Many of these spices are good liver herbs, and the carrot is great too — any root vegetables are good food for the liver. The hot spices will help to get the blood moving and stir things up. A perfect detox recipe."

ROASTED CORN SOUP

The Aztecs believed that corn was the food of the gods. This surprising treatment of a traditional American staple takes corn cooked on the cob to a new, intriguing level.

INGREDIENTS:
8 ears of corn
2 Tbs. + 2 Tbs. extra-
  virgin olive oil
salt and pepper
parsley, chopped

PREPARATION: Preheat oven to 425°F.
Peel off the outer husks of each corn ear, leaving a single layer to cover the kernels. Cut off the top brown edges of the silk.

Brush each ear to cover, using 2 Tbs. of olive oil. Sprinkle lightly with salt and pepper. Bake for 10 minutes. Turn each ear. Bake for another 10 minutes. Remove from the oven and allow to cool. Remove remaining husks and silk. Shave off kernels with a shark knife and set aside.

In a heavy stock pot over medium heat, warm 2 Tbs. oil. Add the garlic, onion and jalapeno. Cook until onion is translucent. Add corn and blend completely. Add broth. Reduce heat to low. Simmer for 20-30 minutes. Remove from heat and allow to cool slightly.

Working in 2-cup batches, puree the soup in a blender. Return pureed ingredients to the stock pot. Stir in the soy milk and warm the soup over a low heat for 10-15 minutes.

Garnish individual servings with a generous sprinkling of chopped parsley.

SERVING SUGGESTION: For a colorful presentation, serve with a basket full or baked corn chips and a dish of salsa.

KALE SOUP

You may recognize the name of this traditional Portuguese one-pot meal, best known for its use of spicy sausage and leafy green kale. Still packed with the nutrition of leafy green vegetables, this version has been modified for Eating Clean.

1½ Tbs. extra-virgin olive oil

1 onion, chopped

2 cloves garlic, minced

8 cups water or a combination of water and organic, preservative-free chicken stock

2 potatoes, peeled, thinly sliced, or

1 cup rice, cooked

2 tsp. salt

¼ tsp. black pepper

½ Tbs. extra-virgin olive oil

8 oz. organic, preservative-free chicken sausage, or

8 oz. chicken breast, cooked

1 tsp. cumin

½ tsp. paprika

4 cups shredded kale, Swiss chard or collard leaves (a combination of any or all of these!), washed and dried

Heat oil in a large stock pot. Add onion and garlic and cook until translucent but not brown. Add water or chicken stock, potatoes or rice, salt and pepper. Cook until potatoes (or rice) are very soft. Remove pot from heat and mash potatoes (or rice) so that they blend with the liquid.

In a separate skillet, heat oil. Add sausage or chicken and spices and cook until browned. Add this to the stock pot. To capture the delicious browned bits in the skillet, pour a cup of the soup stock into the skillet. Gently stir the stock while scraping the skillet bottom. Pour this into the big stock pot also. Simmer for 5 minutes. Add leafy greens to the soup pot. Continue to simmer ingredients for 5-10 minutes. Serve hot.

CREAMY CARROT SOUP

A creamier and less spicey variation than the
SPICY CARROT SOUP on page 92.

2 Tbs. extra-virgin olive
   oil
1 leek, rinsed and sliced

8 carrots, diced

½ tsp. nutmeg
½ tsp. cinnamon
1 Tbs. fresh ginger,
   minced
½ tsp. salt

4–6 cups water, or
vegetable or organic,
   preservative-free
   chicken stock

1 cup soy milk

thyme, fresh (optional)

Heat oil over medium heat in a large stock pot. Add leek and stir to coat thoroughly. Cook for 2 minutes. Toss in the carrots, stirring thoroughly. Continue to cook vegetables for 5 minutes. Add spices and stir to coat vegetables thoroughly. Allow to cook for 2 more minutes over medium-low heat. Cover vegetables with water or stock, and reduce heat to low. Cover soup pot and cook the soup until the carrot chunks are tender and easy to pierce with a fork.

Remove soup from the heat. Allow to cool for 15 minutes. Working in 2-cup batches, puree the soup mixture in the blender. Return pureed ingredients to the soup pot. Add soy milk and heat over low heat for 5 minutes.

Serve and garnish with fresh thyme, if desired.

SALLY'S CHICKEN SOUP

When I found myself discussing recipes within minutes of meeting my new friend, Sally, it was obvious that the idea of clean food — and international cuisine — was taking over my life! Here is a warming soup with a Far East flavor.

½ tsp. curry powder
(page 126)
2 cups chicken broth,
organic and pesticide-
free
½ boneless chicken
breast, skinned and
diced
1 Tbs. corn starch with 1
tsp. water

2 cups coconut milk
(page 20)
½ tsp. lemon rind, freshly
grated

chives, fresh and
chopped
scallions, fresh and
chopped

In a large sauce pan, blend the curry powder with broth. Warm the mixture over medium heat. Add the chicken and continue to heat for 5 more minutes.

Stir in the moistened corn starch and bring mixture to a boil.

Add coconut milk and lemon rind and reduce heat. Stir well. Do not allow the soup to come to a boil again, but keep it cooking on a low simmer until broth thickens..

Ready to serve.
Garnish individual servings with the chives and/or scallions.

SPICEY THAI CHICKEN SOUP

3 cups coconut milk
(page 20)
½ tsp. curry powder
(page 126)
2 stalks lemon grass
(often available now in
the fresh produce sec-
tion of larger supermar-
kets)
3 slices fresh ginger
root, skinned

1 organic, pesticide-free
chicken breast, bone-
less and skinless, cut
into 1" chunks

2 tomatoes, diced
½ tsp. salt

1 Tbsp. parsley,
chopped
1 lime, sliced
½ tsp. hot red-pepper
flakes (optional)

In a lidded stock pot, over a medium-high heat, bring the coconut milk, curry, lemon grass and ginger to a boil for a full minute.

Add the chicken. Reduce heat to medium and allow the chicken to cook for 10-15 minutes (there should not be any pink color to the meat when sliced through).

Add tomatoes and salt. Cook over medium heat for another 2-3 minutes. Remove from heat and serve. (Note: you may want to fish out the ginger slices before serving. They can be quite 'hot' when bitten into!)

Garnish each soup bowl with a sprinkling of pars-ley, a slice of lime, and a few hot red-pepper flakes (if desired).

CHICK PEA SOUP

A culinary treasure from France's Provencal region.

1 cup chick peas,
  cooked
2–3 cloves garlic,
  minced
juice of 2 lemons
4 cups chicken stock,
  organic and preserva-
  tive-free

1 Tbs. fresh parsley,
  chopped
1 Tbs. toasted sesame
  seeds

In a blender, puree the chick peas, garlic, lemon juice, olive oil, and 1-2 cups chicken stock. (as much chicken stock as your blender can comfortably hold). Transfer puree to a large soup pot. Add the remaining chicken stock. Heat gently over medium heat until hot.

Serve immediately. Garnish each soup bowl with a sprinkle of the chopped parsley and a pinch of sesame seeds.

KIDNEY BEAN SOUP

2 Tbs. extra-virgin olive oil

2 cloves garlic, sliced

1 onion, large, sliced

2 cups prepared kidney beans

4 cups vegetable stock

6-8 tomatoes, peeled and diced

1 lemon wedge

1 Tbs. oregano

1 tsp. dill

1 tsp. basil

½ tsp. red pepper

½ tsp. mint, fresh or dried

cooked brown rice or chunks of celery

parsley, chopped

Heat the olive oil. Add the onions and garlic. Cook just until the onions are transparent.

Add the kidney beans, stock and tomatoes. Simmer for 15-30 minutes.

Add the herbs and lemon slice (squeeze in the juice and throw the rind in after it, leaving it to cook, too) and continue cooking for an additional 15 minutes.

Serve with brown rice or chunks of celery cooked in the soup.

LENTIL SOUP

4 cups organic, preservative-free chicken stock
1 cup lentils, dry

2 cloves garlic, chopped
1 onion, medium, sliced
2 stalks celery, chopped
1 carrot, medium, thinly sliced
1½ cups coarsely chopped tomatoes
1 Tbs. extra-virgin olive oil
1 bay leaf

2 tsp. cumin
1 tsp. thyme, dried
2 Tbs. mint, fresh or dried
1 lemon wedge

parsley, freshly chopped
mint, fresh (optional)

Put the lentils and stock in a 4-quart pot and bring to a boil. Boil for about 5 minutes and reduce the heat.

Add the garlic, onion, celery and carrot. Gently stir to mix, then add the tomatoes, olive oil and bay leaf. Simmer for about 20 minutes.

Add the cumin, thyme and mint and simmer for an additional 15-20 minutes. Squeeze the lemon wedge into the pot and put the rind into the soup for the last 5 minutes. Leave it in the pot until the soup has been consumed.

Serve with lots of fresh chopped parsley. If fresh mint is available, add that as a garnish.

BLACK BEAN SOUP

A good choice when serving a group — the quantity is quite large. The original version of this called for bacon and beef broth rather than chicken. Robust flavor is not lost with this cleaner, lighter interpretation.

2 Tbs. extra-virgin olive oil

2 onion, chopped

4 carrots, sliced into coarse rounds

4-6 cloves garlic, minced

8 cups chicken broth, organic and pesticide-free

1 lb. dried black beans, rinsed

½-1 tsp. cayenne pepper

rind of ½ lemon (one long piece)

2 Tbs. red wine vinegar

Heat oil in a large soup pot. Add onion, carrots and garlic. Stir and cook for 10 minutes.

Add 6 cups of the broth, the beans, the cayenne, the lemon rind. Simmer for 2–3 hours, or until beans are tender but not mushy. Discard the lemon rind.

Puree half of the soup.

Return the soup puree to the pot and add the remaining 2 cups of broth and the vinegar. Cook 5 more minutes.

Serve.

SERVING SUGGESTION:

Put ½ cup of rice in the bottom of each bowl before ladling the soup.

CHILLED BEET SOUP

This is a non-traditional, vegetarian variation on the Borscht Soup originally brought to New York City by early Russian immigrants. Because beets are recommended for those following a liver detoxification diet, and because this chilled soup is such a solid Eating Clean offering, I hope you will forgive the poetic license with regards to ingredients.

3 cups water
1 lb. beets, peeled and thinly sliced
1 carrot, large, peeled and sliced
1 clove garlic, minced

2 Tbs. lemon juice, fresh
salt, to taste
Black pepper, a dash or to taste

Soy-based 'sour cream'

Parsley, fresh, finely chopped

In a large stock pot, combine 3 cups of water, beets, carrot and garlic. Bring to a boil. Reduce heat and simmer until beets are tender. Remove from heat.

Into the pot, add lemon juice, salt and pepper. Working in batches, puree the beet soup in a blender. Transfer to a lidded glass container and chill for at least 2 hours.

To serve, garnish each serving with a tablespoon each of dairy-free 'sour cream' and parsley.

CHILLED GAZPACHO

4 cups pureed tomatoes

½ medium onion, grated
2-3 tomatoes, diced
1 green pepper, diced
2 cloves garlic, pressed
1 cucumber, peeled,
  seeded and diced
1 lemon, juice only
1 lime, juice only
¼ cup Parsley, minced
1 tsp. basil, dried, or 3-4
  leaves basil, fresh,
  minced
¼ tsp. cumin
1 Tbs. cilantro, minced
  (optional)
salt and pepper, to taste

In a very large mixing bowl or soup pot, combine all ingredients. Working in batches, puree the mixture in a food processor or blender. Chill and serve.

"The onions, garlic, lemon and parsley are all particularly good for a detox."
— Dr. Sara Thyr

SWEET TREATS

FRESH FRUIT SALAD

Mix your favorite fruits together as the season allows. Create your own favorite blend of colors, flavors and textures. The combination below is simply a suggestion.

½ canteloupe, cut into bite-sized chunks

½ cup organic strawberries, fresh and sliced

1 plum, cut into chunks

1 navel orange, peeled and cut into bite-sized chunks

¼ cup blueberries, fresh

¼ cup raspberries, fresh (optional)

In a medium-sized bowl, mix all of the fruit together. Be sure to include the juice of the orange that escaped as you were cutting it into pieces, too.

FRESH IDEAS FOR FRUIT: Consider preparing fruit salad to accompany hot cereal at breakfast, as a dessert elegant enough for dinner guests, or as a mini-meal to enjoy sometime during the day.

FRUIT & NUT SPREAD

My father created this naturally sweet spread as an answer to his sweet tooth, after health issues forced him to give up sugar. The dense sweetness of the dates, enhanced with cinnamon, cloves and ginger, quickly satisfies a hankering for a treat.

½ cup almonds, finely chopped
½ cup walnuts, finely chopped

½ lb. pitted dates, finely chopped or pureed in a food processor
apple cider
¾ tsp. ginger
½ tsp. cinnamon
pepper
2 pinches cloves

1 apple – any organic type will do, peeled and grated

Combine almonds and walnuts and set aside in a large bowl.

Mix dates with the apple cider, ginger, cinnamon, pepper and cloves. Stir the puree into the nut mixture.

Stir grated apple into the date mixture. Add cider as necessary so that mixture is thick but spreadable.

Spread on rice cakes or wedges of fresh pear for a sweet treat. Add some almond butter, too, and you have your own Eating Clean version of the classic PB&J!

APPLE STRUDELS

It is possible to satisfy a sweet tooth, even when flour and sugar are no longer part of your daily diet. However, these are made with corn tortillas. Corn is a reactive food for many people. Consult your naturopath before including these during a detox.

---

2 Cortland apples (or any other favorite cooking apple),

2 peaches, peeled and sliced

½ cup pineapple, fresh and diced

1 mango, peeled and diced

1 Tbs. golden raisins

2 Tbs. orange juice

½ tsp. pumpkin pie spice, or

- ½ tsp. cinnamon
- ⅛ tsp. nutmeg
- ⅛ tsp. ginger

4 corn tortillas, large (lard-free)

Preheat oven to 425°F. In a heavy sauce pan, place all of the fruits, orange juice and spices. Heat slowly and gently over low heat for 15 minutes, stirring so that the flavors of the fruits and spices meld together.

Fill each tortilla with a scoop of the cooked fruit. Fold over to make an envelope and place it seam-side down on a lightly oiled baking sheet. Bake for 12-15 minutes. Fruits should appear bubbly and piping hot!

APPLE MUFFINS

I particularly enjoy baking. Figuring out how to create home-baked treats that were wheat- and dairy-free was one of the most satisfying experiences of my own first liver detox!

¾ cup xylitol
⅓ cup canola oil
2 eggs, beaten

1 cup spelt flour
½ cup soy flour
1½ tsp. baking powder
½ tsp. salt
⅔ cup soy milk
2 cups apple, peeled and diced
¼ cup raisins (optional)
¼ cup nuts, finely chopped (optional)
2 tsp. cinnamon

Preheat oven to 375°F. Fill a 12-muffin tin with paper liners.

In a large mixing bowl combine xylitol and oil. Add eggs and mix thoroughly.

In another bowl blend together the spelt flour, baking powder, salt and cinnamon. Add this to the egg mixture. Slowly stir in the soy milk. Fold in the apple chunks, raisins and nuts.

Spoon the batter into the muffin cups. Bake for 15-20 minutes, or until muffins are firm to the touch and a skewer comes clean when inserted into a muffin center. Allow muffins to cool on a wire rack before serving.

SERVING SUGGESTION: Slice muffins in half and spread with almond butter. Serve with your favorite green tea.

PUMPKIN MUFFINS

Leftover sweet potatoes or yams also make a good muffin foundation. Simply use sweet potato or yam in place of the pumpkin puree. All other ingredients and quantities remain the same.

---

2 cups spelt flour
1 Tbs. baking powder
½ tsp. baking soda
1 tsp. grated orange zest
½ tsp. salt
¼ tsp. nutmeg
½ tsp. cinnamon
⅛ tsp. ginger

1 cup pureed pumpkin
½ cup xylitol
¼ cup orange juice
1 Tbs. molasses
1 cup soy milk, plain

¼ cup chopped nuts (optional)
¼ cup raisins (optional)

> These muffins are wonderful for eating clean, but not great for a detox, due to the refined carbohydrates. When in doubt about the ingredients of a recipe for your detox, consult your naturopath first.

Preheat oven to 375°F. Line 12 muffin cups with paper liners.

In a large mixing bowl blend flour, baking powder, baking soda, zest, salt, nutmeg, cinnamon and ginger.

In another mixing bowl combine pumpkin puree, xylitol, orange juice and molasses. Stir in soy milk. Gradually stir the wet ingredients into the dry ingredients, working in about ½-cup increments, until blended. Gently fold in nuts and raisins, if desired.

Divide batter into the muffin cups. Bake for 20-25 minutes or until firm. Remove from oven and cool on a wire rack.

Hint: Muffins peel out of paper liners easier if allowed to cool completely beforehand.

ZUCCHINI MUFFINS

These muffins freeze well and provide a great opportunity to make use of a bountiful summer crop of this prolific vegetable.

2 cups zucchini, shredded
3 eggs
1½ cups xylitol
1 cup applesauce (unsweetened)
1 tsp. vanilla extract

2 cups spelt flour
1 cup soy flour
1 tsp. baking powder
1 tsp. baking soda
½ tsp. salt
1 tsp. cinnamon
½ cup chopped nuts
½ cup raisins

Makes 2 dozen!

Preheat oven to 350°F. Fill 24 muffin cups with paper liners.

In a large mixing bowl combine zucchini, eggs, xylitol, applesauce and vanilla.

In another large bowl blend the spelt and soy flours, baking powder, baking soda, salt, cinnamon, nuts and raisins.

Gradually stir wet ingredients into dry, adding ½-cup at a time. Distribute the batter evenly amongst the 24 muffin cups. Bake for 20-25 minutes or until muffins are firm.

DIPS,
DRESSINGS
& SPICES

BASIC VINAIGRETTE DRESSING

2 garlic cloves, pressed
¼ tsp. salt

¼ cup rice vinegar
¼ cup balsamic vinegar
1 tsp. Dijon mustard
  (optional)
1 tsp. basil, dried or
  fresh and minced
¼ tsp. oregano, dried or
  fresh and minced
salt and pepper, to taste

1 cup extra-virgin olive
  oil

In a small bowl, mash together the garlic and salt until it they are blended into a paste.

Transfer garlic mixture to a glass far with a tight-fitting lid. Add vinegars, mustard, basil, oregano, salt and pepper. Shake thoroughly to blend all ingredients.

Add olive oil. Shake again until all of the ingredients are blended and smooth.

Use immediately. Refrigerate leftovers.

LIME VINAIGRETTE DRESSING

2 garlic cloves, pressed
¼ tsp. salt

¼ cup rice vinegar
¼ cup lime juice, fresh
1 tsp. Dijon mustard
  (optional)
salt and pepper to taste

1 cup extra-virgin olive oil

In a small bowl, mash together the garlic and salt until they are blended into a paste.

Transfer garlic mixture to a glass jar with a tight-fitting lid. Add vinegar, lime juice, mustard, salt and pepper. Shake thoroughly to blend all ingredients.

Add olive oil. Shake again until all of the ingredients are blended and smooth.

Use immediately. Refrigerate leftovers.

MANDARIN DRESSING

1 garlic clove, pressed
1 slice fresh ginger,
  minced
⅓ cup rice vinegar
⅓ cup orange juice

½ cup oil (flax seed or
  extra-virgin olive)
2 tsp. sesame oil

In a lidded jar combine
garlic, ginger, vinegar
and orange juice.

Shake thoroughly to blend
all ingredients.

Add oils. Shake again
until all of the ingredients
are blended and smooth.

Chill before using.
Refrigerate leftovers.

TAHINI DRESSING

½ cup balsamic vinegar
½ cup rice vinegar
2 Tbs. lemon juice, fresh
2 cloves garlic, pressed
½ tsp. salt
dash of black pepper

½ cup sesami tahini
1½ cup extra-virgin olive
  oil

In a mixing bowl combine the vinegars, lemon juice, garlic, salt and pepper. Pour into a blender.

Slowly add tahini and then olive oil, all the while keeping the blender on the lowest possible speed. (Tip: Pour these ingredients through the hole in the blender lid usually used for the lifting knob. This will eliminate potential mess, should the blender be inclined to spray mixture!)

Use immediately for salad dressing or raw vegetable dipping sauce.

Store leftovers in refrigerator in a covered glass container.

MORE TAHINI DRESSING!

"This tahini dressing recipe is a favorite hand-me-down. It's wonderful on steamed veggies, almost any fish, and chicken, too. We always have some in the fridge. I suggest using olive oil rather than any other type of cooking oil." — Dr. Sara Thyr

½–⅓ cup wheat-free tamari sauce
¼ cup lemon juice, fresh
5 Tbsp. sesame tahini

1½ cup extra-virgin olive oil
2 tsp. dill, chopped
2–3 cloves garlic, minced

In a blender, whir together the tamari, lemon juice and tahini.

Slowly drizzle in the olive oil, a little at a time. Add dill and garlic.

Enjoy!

TAPENADE

If you love olives, you're going to love this! Delicious when spread on crackers or used as a seasoning, such as tossed with Ratatouille (see page 73).

7 oz. pitted black Greek olives

1 Tbs. capers

2–3 anchovies

3 Tbs. extra-virgin olive oil

¼ cup water

Blend all ingredients together at once in a food processor. Final consistency should be that of a paste.

Tapenade is a bit salty for a detox. It is a tasty indulgence to be enjoyed in moderation when eating clean, though.

AVOCADO DIP (GUACAMOLE)

2 ripe avocados

1 lemon
2 cloves garlic, pressed
1 tomato, finely minced
½ onion, grated
¼–½ tsp. salt

In a medium-sized mixing bowl, use a fork to mash the meat of the two avocados. If they are ripe enough, this should be very easy and quick.

Add the juice of the lemon, the pressed garlic, tomato and onion. Taste first before seasoning with salt!

SUGGESTED SERVING: Use jacama slices for dipping. They're a clean, vegetable alternative to corn chips! Jacama can be found in the tropical vegetable section of larger supermarkets.

DR. THYR recommends: "Avocados are at the top of the Environmental Working Group's list of the 12 least contaminated fruits and vegetables. Therefore, save your organic dollars for foods such as peppers or spinach!"

EGGPLANT SPREAD

In Middle Eastern restaurants you'll see this offered as
BABA GANOUJ.

2 eggplants, medium-sized

2–3 Tbs. lemon juice, fresh
⅓ cup sesame tahini
3 cloves garlic, minced
1 tsp. salt

Preheat oven to 400 °F. Lightly oil a cookie sheet or any 9x13 roasting pan. Rinse off the outer skins of the egg plant and slice off the stem end of each. With a kitchen fork, gently prick the eggplant skins. Set them on the pan and roast for about 45 minutes. They should be completely cooked through and look utterly deflated.

Scoop out the insides of the eggplant into a mixing bowl. Add lemon juice, sesame tahini, garlic, salt and olive oil. Mash and blend ingredients with a potato masher. Consistency will be soft and spreadable. Chill in a lidded container before serving. Use as a sandwich spread or a tasty dip for fresh vegetables.

HUMUS: CHICK PEA DIP or SPREAD

2 cups chick peas prepared using the method described on page 59.

2-4 cloves garlic, pressed (allow your passion for garlic to dictate quantity)

¼ cup freshly squeezed lemon juice

½ cup sesame tahini

¼ cup parsley leaves, finely minced

1 Tbs. extra virgin olive oil

¼ organic sweet red pepper, diced

1 scallion stalk, finely sliced

Using a food processor or blender, combine chick peas, garlic, lemon juice, tahini oil and parsley. Blend thoroughly so that you now have a thick, paste-like consistency. Transfer to a lidded container and chill before serving.

Garnish with scallions and sweet red peppers and serve as a dip with sticks of celery and carrot, slices of green and sweet red pepper, or peeled and sliced jacama.

A
WORD ON LEMON AND PARSLEY
"Lemon is a good addition to a detox diet for its many liver benefits and the increased acidity of the GI tract. (Note: it is better for increasing acidity when taken alone). Parsley is known to be a good alterative; it is tonifying to the blood."
– DR. SARA THYR

SALSA FRESCA

Homemade with fresh ingredients, this beats anything bought off the shelf.

1 white or red onion, small, finely chopped, rinsed and drained

2 Tbs. lime juice, fresh

2 large tomatoes, seeded and diced

¼–½ cup cilantro, minced (amount determined by your particular taste preference)

3-5 jalapeno peppers, fresh, seeded and minced (adjust number of peppers to suit your taste)

6 radishes, finely diced

1 clove garlic, minced

¼ tsp. salt

NOTE: Be sure to rinse your diced onion! Doing so will remove the biting aftertaste that could interfere with the successful marriage of flavors in your Salsa Fresca!

In a mixing bowl, toss the onion with the lime juice. Set aside.

In another bowl, combine the remaining ingredients. Then add the onion mix. Stir well.

Can be served immediately or stored in the refrigerator, covered, for up to 5 days.

PACIFIC RIM DIPPING SAUCE

Dress up a grilled chicken dinner or serve as a dipping sauce for **Artichokes Divine** (find the recipe page 63).

½ cup organic, sugar-free peanut butter, smooth variety

2 tsp. wheat-free soy sauce

2 tsp. balsamic vinegar

¾-cup water

1 Tbs. lemon juice, fresh

2 cloves garlic, minced

In a small but deep-sided bowl, whisk together all of the ingredients. Cover and set aside for 2 hours to give the various flavors time to meld and marry. Then, serve.

NOTE: Leftover sauce should be refrigerated.

CURRY POWDER
Homemade

There are many tasty and full-bodied curry powders available and ready to use. However, if you're feeling particularly adventurous and have a desire to put your signature on some of your spicy preparations, try your hand at blending your own curry powder. Store it in an airtight container. Share some with friends. Create your own innovations!

---

4 tsp. coriander
2 tsp. turmeric
1 tsp. cumin
1 tsp. dry mustard
1 tsp. ginger
1 tsp. chili powder
1 tsp. cinnamon
1 tsp. cardamon
½ tsp. pepper

Place all ingredients in a small mixing bowl and blend thoroughly.

Store in an airtight jar or zip-lock bag.

Yield: 4 Tbs.

RESOURCES

&

INFORMATION for

EATING CLEAN

Why Eat Organic?

What does organic mean and is it worth the extra expense? In order for a farm to qualify as "organic", there must not have been any prohibited fertilizers and/or pesticides applied there within the last three years, according to the United States Department of Agriculture. Farmers growing organic fruits and vegetables must rely on birds, insects and other organisms to combat pests and diseases. Meat, chicken, poultry and eggs that are labeled as "organic" come from animals that have not been given any antibiotics or growth hormones.

Organic foods cost more. Sometimes it is necessary to travel an extra distance to search out organic foods. They can be inconvenient on the pocketbook as well as one's lifestyle. And until recently there's been some question as to how reliable is organic labelling.

However, beginning in October of this year, national standards will be in place, offering the consumer a measure of confidence about foods being sold as organic. In order to distribute produce and animal products as organic, farms must be certified by a U.S.D.A.-accredited agency. Any food labelled "100% organic" must be only organic. If a food is labelled "organic", then its ingredients must be least 95% organic.

Making changes to incorporate more organically raised foods into one's diet will certainly reduce the amount of pesticide residues consumed and hopefully reap long-term health benefits. There is still a lot of disagreement between different health and medical professionals as to the ultimate damage that these chemicals cause to our bodies. But if you're reading this book, you're already interested in eliminating potentially harmful pesticides from your diet! Eating cleaner can only enhance one's health.

Take a look, below, at the Environmental Working Group's list of what they call The Dirty Dozen. With this list in mind, it is recommended that organic fruits and vegetables be used to prepare the recipes in this book, as often as possible. If you are trying to eat 'cleaner' than you have in the past, you must be thinking 'organic' now. Look for chickens in the meat department of your grocery that have been raised in a free-range setting and without growth hormone injections. Eggs from free-range chickens are becoming more common at mainstream supermarkets, too. Organic beef may require more research than eggs and chickens. Check with your naturopath for a resource recommendation.

Environmental Working Group's Dirty Dozen
Most Contaminated Fruits & Vegetables:

1. Strawberries	7. Celery
2. Bell Peppers	8. Apples
3. Spinach	9. Apricots
4. Cherries (U.S.)	10. Green Beans
5. Peaches	11. Chilean Grapes
6. Canteloupe (Mex.)	12. Cucumbers

Least Contaminated Fruits & Vegetables:

1. Avocado	7. U.S. Grapes
2. Corn	8. Bananas
3. Onion	9. Plums
4. Sweet Potato	10. Green Onions
5. Cauliflower	11. Watermelon
6. Brussels Sprouts	12. Broccoli

Environmental Working Group is a non-profit research organization.

LIVER FOODS

Recommended during a detox and for general clean eating

- Artichokes

- Garlic

- Parsley

- Lemon

- Onions

- Beets

- Whey Protein
  (assists in elimination
  of toxins)

PANTRY

Must-Haves

- Extra-virgin olive oil
- Garlic
- Onions
- Tomatoes
- Rice
- Beans, Beans, Beans
- Bell Peppers: Green, Yellow & Red – organic, of course
- Chicken Broth, homemade from organic, range-free, pesticide-free chickens, stored in batches in the freezer
- Hot Cereal
- Soy & Nut Milks

- 1 heavy skillet or wok
- 1 large soup pot
- 1 blender

SPIRULINA:
The Green Food

Spirulina is good for cleansing because of its rich chlorophyll content. It is easy to absorb and thus good for people who have poor nutrient assimilation. The plant protein in spirulina is also very digestible. Another benefit is that spirulina will also decrease cravings for animal protein. It is tonifying to the liver and protects the kidneys against injury that occurs from taking medications. (Pitchford) Spirulina has also been shown to prevent cancer formation and increase mental capacity. (Pitchford) It is very high in GLA, gammalinolenic acid, which has a wealth of health benefits.

Wheat, barley grass and chorella are also green foods that contain large amounts of chlorophyll. Barley grass is more readily digestible than wheat, and a popular choice for those who are sensitive to wheat products. Barley grass is also a good choice because it contains many digestive enzymes that can help rid the body of toxic substances in food. The superoxide dismutase (SOD) can help rid the body of free radicals.

Consult your naturopath or nutrition professional for specific brand recommendations.

— Dr. Sara Thyr

OTHER RESOURCES

ONLINE:

www.bastyr.edu
find out more about naturopathic medicine

www.naturopathic.org
locate a naturopathic doctor in your neighborhood, or learn
more about naturopathic medicine

www.foodnews.org
learn about pesticides in our food

BIBLIOGRAPHY

Crinnion, Walter, ND. Unpublished conference information.

Pitchford, Paul. <u>Healing with Whole Foods.</u> 1993. North Atlantic Books. Berkley, CA.

McGee, Harold. <u>On Food and Cooking: The science and lore of the kitchen.</u> 1984. Fireside. New York, NY.

Lee, John R., MD. "Medical Letter". Monthly publication. May 2002: Xylitol. Phoenix, AZ.

INDEX

Index continued

Index continued

Index continued

Index continued

❦ MORNING GLORY PRESS
QUICK ORDER FORM

email orders: admin@a-zmarketing.com

web site: www.a-zmarketing.com

postal orders: MORNING GLORY PRESS
                   PO Box 373
                   Nashua NH 03061-0373

Please send the following:

_____ **EATING CLEAN** $19.95

_____ Total Quantity X $19.95 each . . .$ _____

Shipping & Handling:

$4.00 for the first book;

$2.00 each additional. . . . .$ _____

TOTAL . . . .$ _____

Payment: ❏ Check ❏ Credit Card

❏ VISA ❏ MasterCard ❏ AmEx ❏ Discover

Card number: _____

Name on Card: _____

Expiration Date: _____

Thank you for your order.

Orders paid by credit card shipped within 3 business days.